MAGDALENE DE LANCEY was born in the Scottish Lowlands in 1793 into an intellectual family who played a significant role in the Scottish Enlightenment. In 1815, just as Napoleon escaped from Elba, she married Sir William De Lancey, one of the British Army's first professional officers. Sir William was appointed the Duke of Wellington's Chief of Staff and, as preparations were made for battle, she accompanied her husband to Brussels. She was eventually to nurse him through his last days on the edge of the battlefield at Waterloo.

ANDREW ROBERTS took a first class honours degree in Modern History at Gonville & Caius College, Cambridge, where he is an honorary senior scholar. He is the author of numerous books that include the critically acclaimed *Napoleon and Wellington* (2001) and *Waterloo: Napoleon's Last Gamble* (2005). He appears regularly on British television and radio, and writes for *The Sunday Telegraph*, *The Spectator*, *Literary Review*, *Mail on Sunday* and *The Daily Telegraph*. He is married and lives in London.

RUTH FULLER-SESSIONS is Magdalene De Lancey's great-great-great-great niece – Magdalene's brother Basil Hall was her great-great-great grandfather. She read Classics at St. Hilda's College, Oxford and is now Head of Production at Atlantic Productions, an independent television production company in London, which specialises in historical documentaries.

A Week At Waterloo

by Magdalene De Lancey

Introduced by Andrew Roberts
With a Foreword by Ruth Fuller-Sessions

REPORTAGE PRESS DESPATCHES

REPORTAGE PRESS

Published by Reportage Press
26 Richmond Way, London W12 8LY United Kingdom
Tel: 0044 (0)7971 461 935 — E-mail: info@reportagepress.com
http://www.reportagepress.com

A Week At Waterloo was produced under the
editorial direction of Rosie Whitehouse.

British Library Cataloguing in Publication Data.
A catalogue record for this book is available from the British
Library. ISBN-13: 978-0-9555729-8-2

Cover design and layout by Joshua Haymann, Paris.

Printed and bound in Great Britain by Antony Rowe Ltd,
Chippenham, Wiltshire. www.antonyrowe.co.uk

Magdalene De Lancey originally wrote this account of her experiences at Waterloo for her brother, Captain Basil Hall, who was a well-known author and had been a close friend of her husband. The original manuscript has been lost but copies exist that were made by the author and members of the family, which were then circulated to friends, including the authors Charles Dickens and Sir Walter Scott. There also exists a far shorter abridged version of the account from which all personal details have been cut. The version reprinted here originally appeared in *A Week At Waterloo* published by John Murray in 1906.

The letters from Sir Walter Scott and Charles Dickens to Captain Basil Hall were originally printed in the *Century Magazine* (New York), April 1906 and reproduced in *A Week At Waterloo* (1906). The letter from Scott has since disappeared but the letter from Dickens is now held in the collection at the Huntington Library in California. It is reproduced with their permission.

Rosie Whitehouse
London 2008

Magdalene De Lancey (née Hall) was clearly a highly remarkable woman. To have decided to accompany her husband, Colonel Sir William Howe De Lancey, to the campaign against the Emperor Napoleon I of France in the Austrian Netherlands (present-day Belgium) was brave; to have scarcely left his side as she nursed him for a week as he lay mortally wounded after the battle of Waterloo was magnificent, but to have written about the whole terrifying and moving experience so honestly and engagingly was also invaluable. She has been compared to her contemporary Jane Austen transported onto a battlefield, and her *Narrative* certainly evokes the Brussels scene from William Makepeace Thackeray's *Vanity Fair*.

A daughter of the Scottish Enlightenment, Magdalene Hall came from a family distinguished both socially and intellectually. Her father Sir James Hall (1761-1832), was the fourth baronet of Dunglass in East Lothian, and a noted geologist and inventor; he proved that limestone could form marble without decomposition, if subjected to considerable pressure during heating. He has been described as 'That relatively rare specimen of early-nineteenth-century life: the intellectual aristocrat.'[1] Before Cambridge and Edinburgh universities, Sir James attended the Brienne Military Academy at the same time as the young Napoleon Bonaparte, who remembered him well in later life. He subsequently studied volcanoes in Europe, sat as an MP during the Napoleonic Wars, and served as a highly respected president of the Royal Society of Edinburgh.

In 1786, Sir James married Lady Helen Hamilton Douglas, the daughter of Dunbar Douglas, 4th Earl of Selkirk (1722-1799), who had supported the Government during the 1745 Jacobite Rebellion and whose marriage to Hon. Margaret Home began the Douglas-Home dynasty, which produced the twentieth-century Prime Minister, Sir Alec Douglas-Home. As well as having intellect on her paternal side of the family and aristocratic lineage on her maternal, Magdalene's brother Basil - author, traveller, intellectual, friend of Sir Walter Scott and naval captain - was also a very considerable figure in his own right. He was present at the death of Sir John Moore at Corunna and interviewed Napoleon on St Helena, before dying in a Portsmouth lunatic asylum in 1844. Magdalene herself was accurately described by a friend, William Hay, as 'an amiable, kind and beautiful young woman'.[2]

William De Lancey (also spelt Delancey, De Lancy and Delancy) came from a New York military family of Huguenot descent, hence the French name. His grandfather had been a general and his father Stephen was lieutenant-colonel of the 1st New Jersey Loyal Volunteers, and thus found himself on the losing side of the American War of Independence. Forced to flee the nascent United States after the British defeat, Stephen De Lancey became Governor of Tobago. Born some time between 1778 and 1781, his son William also joined the Army, obtaining a cornetcy in the 16th Light Dragoons in 1792, at the abnormally young age of between eleven and fourteen. Helped by an uncle, General Oliver De Lancey, he became a lieutenant the following year.[3]

Seventeen ninety-three saw the start of the French Revolutionary and Napoleonic Wars, which were only to end – with the exception of a single twelve-months of peace in 1802-3 – twenty-two years later at Waterloo. For almost his entire adult life, therefore, William De Lancey knew only war. In 1795, he was transferred to the 80th Regiment of Foot and sent out to the East Indies, where he stayed for four years learning the military trade in the Mahratta Wars. Unsurprisingly for one with soldiering in the blood and good connections in the military, he rose rapidly, especially once he was attached to the campaign of Sir Arthur Wellesley (later the Duke of Wellington) in the Peninsular in 1809. He showed remarkable bravery at the crossing of the River Douro and the capture of Oporto that year, at the siege and capture of Ciudad Rodrigo in 1811, and at the battle of Vittoria in 1813, after which he was appointed Deputy Quartermaster-General.[4] He was also made a Knight Commander of the Bath when peace came in April 1814. Or what everyone at the time believed to be peace.

It was therefore as a brave, distinguished, unmarried, handsome, titled war hero in his late-thirties, with the publicly expressed confidence of the Commander-in-Chief and every prospect of future advancement, that Sir William De Lancey was posted to the Army cantonment at Edinburgh, where he met Magdalene Hall.

The Halls lived in George Street in Edinburgh and on their nine thousand-acre Dunglass estate near Dunbar, where De Lancey was invited to visit in December 1814. It was something of a whirlwind romance, in that De Lancey proposed soon afterwards, the marriage banns were read in March and the wedding took place on Tuesday, 4 April 1815. Although the marriage worked socially and financially very well for both sides - an ever-present aspect of all Society nuptial alliances of the day – it is very clear from the *Narrative* that this was also a genuine love-match.

Yet the De Lanceys' honeymoon at Dun-glass was immediately cut short by international events. As the marriage banns were being read, Napoleon escaped from Elba, then the Allied Coalition of Britain, Austria, Russia and Prussia denounced the Emperor as an 'outlaw' who would not be permitted to retain the throne of France, and then Louis XVIII suddenly fled Paris. It was said that Napoleon sat down to eat the dinner at the Tuileries palace that had been cooked for the King. In order to keep his throne, the Emperor rebuilt his army and decided to march north on 12 June in order to take Brussels and fling the Anglo-Allied army stationed there off the Continent altogether.

The week of the De Lanceys' wedding also saw Wellington leave Vienna, where he had been acting as the British plenipotentiary at the international Congress assembled there, and take up command of the Anglo-Allied forces at Brussels. He sacked his Quartermaster-General, Napoleon's future gaoler on St Helena, General Sir Hudson Lowe, and appointed De Lancey in his place, at least until Wellington's old Peninsular War Quartermaster, George Murray, could get back from Canada, where he was governor-general. The removal of Lowe created a difficult family situation, since Lowe was married to De Lancey's sister, Susan.

It was uncommon, though certainly not unknown, for wives to follow their husbands to war in those days.[5] Brussels was a friendly capital, and the campaign had broken upon the settled social life there, but it had not led to a mass exodus, at least until it was discovered for certain late on 15 June 1815 that it was Napoleon's next target. There had always been a large British community there; indeed Wellington himself had lived in Brussels as a child, as a cost-cutting measure of his mother's. According to Lady De Lancey's *Narrative*, there was a feeling that the campaign against Napoleon 'might last months', and so on 8 June 1815 the adventurous, newly-wed Magdalene De Lancey arrived in Brussels and took up residence on the third or fourth floors of the house of the Comte de Lannoy at the Impasse du Parc, close to the residence occupied by Wellington himself.

As is also clear from the *Narrative*, in the week between her arrival in Brussels on 8 June and the French army crossing the River Meuse and advancing on Brussels on 15 June, Magdalene and Sir William were somehow able to find plenty of time to entertain, enjoy one another's company and go walking in the park. His duties were nonetheless immense. He was responsible for all matters such as quartering the troops, storing and moving ammunition, drafting orders, victualling the sixty-eight thousand-strong heterogeneous Anglo-Allied army, ensuring that all military equipment was with the right units at the right time, and feeding the horses of a vast cavalry contingent, amongst very many other lesser duties.[6] Lady De Lancey's comment in the *Narrative* that 'Fortunately, my husband had scarcely any business to do, and he only went to the office for about an hour a day' is astonishing in that context. The really frenzied activities at the Allied HQ only began, however, once the news was confirmed that the enormous French *Grande Armée* of 130,000 men was only a matter of fifty miles away.

Although the De Lanceys were invited to the Duchess of Richmond's famous ball on the night of Thursday 15 June, they seem not to have attended. De Lancey himself was at a pre-ball dinner given by the Spanish Ambassador, General d'Alava, when the news arrived of the Emperor's attack. Colonel Augustus Frazer of the Royal Horse Artillery wrote home that day to say, 'I find on my table an invitation to dine with Delancey tomorrow; his lady is here; this will be a pleasanter way of passing the day than marching to Mons.' That evening, however, he added: 'I have just learned that the Duke moves in half an hour. The commander of the Royal Artillery, Sir George Wood thinks to Waterloo, which we cannot find on the map: this is the old story again. I have sent to Delancey's office, where we shall learn the real name, etc. The whole place is in a bustle.'[7]

Part of that bustle, so atmospherically described in *Vanity Fair*, included Lady De Lancey being packed off to Antwerp. After all, Napoleon might win the coming battle, as he had sixty-two of his sixty-nine battles so far, capture Brussels, and intern the British community in north-western Europe. Sir William understandably wanted his new wife at a Channel port rather than facing the rapine and pillage that sometimes followed great sieges of the day. (Napoleon had somewhat hubristically ordered his Imperial Guard to include their ceremonial uniforms in their packs, to wear in the victory parade through the streets of Brussels the day after he brought Wellington to battle.)

De Lancey was meanwhile at the heart of the decision-making apparatus around Wellington in the crucial hours between the evening of Thursday 15 June and his wounding at about 3pm on the afternoon of Sunday the eighteenth. Some historians have even credited the colonel with choosing the slopes of Mont St Jean on which the battle was fought, although this vital decision is more usually accorded to Wellington himself, who knew the ground intimately.

(It must also be mentioned that one revisionist historian has accused De Lancey of being complicit in deliberately misleading the Prussians allies about the true dispositions of the Anglo-Allied

Army at 7am on 16 June 1815. The controversy is a complicated one, but can be followed in Peter Hofschroer's *1815: The Waterloo Campaign* (1998), David Miller's *Lady De Lancey at Waterloo* (Appendix D), and several other journal articles containing various rebuttals and counter-rebuttals. All that we have from the *Narrative* about these issues is Lady De Lancey's comment of her husband that 'the violent exertion requisite to setting the whole army in motion quite stupefied him sometimes'.)

Ensign Howell Rees Gronow of the Guards was surprised and impressed on the morning of Waterloo when 'we heard the trampling of horses' feet, and on looking round perceived a large cavalcade of officers coming at full speed. In a moment we recognized the Duke himself at their head.' Along with the Duke of Richmond, the Prince of Orange and Lord Fitzroy Somerset, Gronow spotted De Lancey riding with the Duke, and noted how: 'They all seemed as gay and unconcerned as if they were riding out to meet the hounds in some quiet English county.' De Lancey clearly understood the importance of maintaining high morale as a key ingredient of leadership in warfare.

The Acting-Quartermaster-General was still riding close to Wellington that afternoon when he was hit by the ricochet of a 'spent' cannonball, which smashed into his back and flung him out of his saddle so violently that Wellington later told his friend Earl Stanhope that he had 'bounded up into the air again like a struck pheasant'.[8]

On another occasion, speaking to the banker and poet Samuel Rogers, Wellington told the whole story. 'De Lancey was with me, and speaking to me when he was struck,' he recalled.

> We were on a point of land that overlooked the plain. I had just been warned off by some soldiers … when a ball came bounding along *en ricochet*, as it is called, striking him on the back, sending him many yards over the head of his horse. He fell on his face, and bounded upwards and fell again. All the Staff dismounted and ran up to him, and when I came up he said, 'Pray tell them to leave me and let me die in peace.'[9]

Wellington ordered De Lancey to be conveyed to the village of Waterloo, whereupon the Staff lost contact with him.[10] No fewer than half of the Staff officers in Wellington's immediate entourage at Waterloo were killed or wounded during the battle. The Prince of Orange was badly wounded by a musket ball; Fitzroy Somerset lost an arm; Sir Alexander Gordon and Colonel Charles Fox Canning were fatally injured, and many others were similarly treated. Wellington himself put his own survival that day down to 'the finger of Providence' being upon him.

Writing his famous report of the battle to Earl Bathurst the day after the battle, the Duke listed De Lancey as 'killed by a cannon shot in the middle of the action', whereas in fact he was lying mortally wounded only yards away in a separate dwelling in the same village.[11] It was easy for Wellington to have assumed De Lancey was dead, and this partly explains the confusing and contradictory rumours that Magdalene was to receive over the following days before she reached his bedside.

The very day after pronouncing him dead, Wellington discovered the truth and visited De Lancey on Tuesday 20 June, finding him in 'a barn' on his return from Brussels, and joking with him that after he pulled through his injury, he would 'have the advantage of Sir Condy in *Castle Rackrent* – you will know what your friends said of you after you were dead'. 'I hope I shall,' De Lancey replied to the Duke's reference of Maria Edgeworth's 1800 satirical novel against Anglo-Irish landlords, in which Sir Condy Rackrent faked his own funeral in order to overhear his friends' opinion of him. 'Poor fellow!' Wellington said later of De Lancey: 'We knew each other ever since we were boys. But I had no time to be sorry. I went on with the army, and never saw him again.' Wellington years later said that De Lancey 'was an excellent officer, and would have risen to great distinction had he lived', and Frazer reported that De Lancey was 'one of [Wellington's] favourite officers; and I believe that the Duke felt his death more than that of anyone else.' Historians have wondered how Wellington, who was born in 1769 and went to Eton, could have been a boyhood friend of De Lancey, who was born a decade later and went to Harrow, but the reference is probably to the period both spent in India in the late 1790s.

The cause of De Lancey's death is a matter that Wellington's assiduous interlocutor alludes to in the Waterloo section of his memoirs, *Recollections of Samuel Rogers*, where he states that it was 'the wind of the shot' that proved fatal, not metal from the cannonball itself, since the skin on De Lancey's back 'remained unbroken'. Magdalene herself ascribes inflammation of the lungs and subsequent water in the chest, which is consistent. It is impossible at this distance of time to know whether modern battlefield medical techniques might have saved him, or to tell whether the leeches and the application of a 'blister' would have done much good under the circumstances of the severe trauma of the torso, especially once 'his breathing was like choking'. For all that he seemed to be improving occasionally during the week after Waterloo, De Lancey was probably doomed from the moment he was hit.

Read purely as a piece of reportage, Magdalene's account is remarkable for the English used – 'my breath was like screaming', she writes - as well as the powerful impact on her senses, such as the smell of gunpowder even ten miles away from

Brussels, and 'the smell of corruption' (i.e. rotting flesh both animal and human) on the battlefield itself. The reversals of fortune, as she first thinks her beloved husband killed, then saved, then killed, then wounded, and so on, are profoundly moving. Sir William De Lancey was buried in the Evere cemetery, three miles north-east of Brussels.[12] Magdalene's *Narrative*, which was written for family and friends rather than a wider audience, remained unpublished until 1888, when it appeared in an abridged version in Britain. Some people had read it by then in manuscript form, such as Charles Dickens, who commented: 'If I live for fifty years, I shall dream of it every now and then, from this hour to the day of my death, with the most frightful reality.' It was published in full in an American magazine in 1906 and later that year another edition appeared, with a commentary by Major B.R. Ward.[13]

More than a century later, with this fine new edition of Lady De Lancey's *Narrative*, Reportage Press will delight *cognoscenti* of early nineteenth century prose, as well as general readers with a feeling for true romance and tragedy, and of course all *aficionados* of the Napoleonic Wars.

Andrew Roberts
Author: *Napoleon and Wellington* and *Waterloo: Napoleon's Last Gamble*
www.andrew-roberts.net

Notes

[1]   Nick Foulkes Dancing into Battle: A Social History of Waterloo p.125

[2]   William Hay, Reminiscences 1808-1815 p.202-3

[3]   Dictionary of National Biography vol V p.755

[4]   Col. John Gurwood, Despatches of the Duke of Wellington vols III p.229, V p.476 and VI p.542

[5]   See Richard Holmes, Redcoat: The British Soldier in the Age of Horse and Musket, passim

[6]   Peter Hofschröer, 1815: The Waterloo Campaign p.138

[7]   ed Ian Fletcher, The Waterloo Campaign p.64

[8]   Stanhope, Notes of Conversations with the Duke of Wellington p.136

[9]   Samuel Rogers, Recollections of Samuel Rogers p.233

[10] Elizabeth Longford, Wellington: The Years of the Sword p.483

[11] John Gurwood, Dispatches of the Duke of Wellington vol VIII pp.146-50

[12] See Miller, Lady De Lancey at Waterloo Chapter XII

[13] Ibid, p.xvi

By Ruth Fuller-Sessions

A Week at Waterloo is the story of a newly – and very happily – married Magdalene De Lancey, who travels to Brussels and the Battle of Waterloo with her army officer husband. When she hears he has been wounded on the first day of the battle, she seeks him out on the battlefield and nurses him in a cottage nearby until he dies from his wounds ten days later. It is told in her own words, as an account for her friends and family of those terrible times.

I first read her narrative as a teenager, out of a sense of duty, because I'd found out it was written by someone in my mother's family. I was expecting something inaccessible and old-fashioned. Instead, I read it in one go and cried myself to sleep.

Magdalene was only twenty-two when the Battle of Waterloo happened, and had been married for just three months to thirty-eight-year-old William De Lancey. It was a whirlwind romance. William was a catch – a successful army officer, the Duke of Wellington's right hand man and Chief of Staff at Waterloo. Unusually, he had been born in New York into one of America's most prominent families, once one of the richest in the world; they had lost everything and had had to settle in England after supporting George III in the American War of Independence. Magdalene, daughter of a baronet, granddaughter of an Earl, was from an intellectual, cultured and wealthy Scottish family.

The background to the events in her story is hard to comprehend today – a wife following her husband abroad to war, officers dancing all through the night before a battle – yet Magdalene's voice comes down through time loud and clear and so modern in its clarity and openness about her great happiness with her husband, and her loss, that at times the contemporary touches seem almost unexpected: she travels with servants and a maid; De Lancey goes to see the Duke to make plans for battle and finds him in his undershirt and slippers, dressing for the Duchess of Richmond's ball as he pores over a map with a Prussian officer in full dress uniform; horses scream in fear as they pick their way through the dead after battle; Magdalene applies leeches to her wounded husband's side and 'foments' his limbs.

Magdalene's capability and practicality are extraordinary. It's worth remembering that as her husband was a Staff Officer who'd survived countless campaigns, she'd have expected he was out of the line of fire, planning the battle with Wellington; she would never have expected him to be injured, or die.

The very real love and respect Magdalene and her husband had for each other are striking. She writes, 'I cannot recollect a day of my short married life that was not perfect'. Theirs seems to have been a relationship between people who saw themselves as equals – one that would be impressive today for its openness, tenderness and closeness, and which stayed strong in awful circumstances. He comes across, not so much as a military man, but as a loving husband; she as a highly intelligent, strong, brave and loving woman. Perhaps some of her practicality and toughness was in her background; both traits seem to have been present in her formidable mother and grandmother. Lady Helen Hall, Magdalene's mother, ran the family estate, Dunglass, while her husband and Magdalene's father, Sir James, was on Royal Society business, conducting scientific experiments or preparing speeches for parliament. Lady Helen had been brought up by her own father, the Earl of Selkirk, to believe women should be left money in their own right, in case wastrel husbands came along to take advantage, and made sure that this was the case with her daughters. However, she considered her own husband a worthy recipient of her own funds,

helping him out when he was strapped for cash
by the cost of rebuilding Dunglass. Magdalene's
grandmother, the Countess of Selkirk, once
saw off John Paul Jones, the Scottish born pi-
rate-turned-founder of the American Navy, who
came to take Magdalene's grandfather, the Earl,
hostage and stole the family silver instead. Her
father, Sir James, was a kind and beloved man,
who had a very close relationship with his wife
and children. Unusually for his time, he considered the education of his daughters a priority,
sending them from Scotland to boarding school
in faraway Bristol. He was a man of wide in-
terests − a scientist, long-time President of the
Royal Society of Scotland, an amateur architect,
a leading early figure in geology and, for a time,
an MP − and also a great entertainer and an excellent dancer.

This is also a story of strange coincidences
that link the families of Magdalene and her husband with that of Napoleon and prove quite
how small the world could be for the privileged
classes in the early nineteenth century. While on
the Grand Tour from 1783 to 1785, Sir James
stayed with his cousin William Hamilton at his
chateau in France (the Hamiltons had had to flee
Scotland after William's father had supported the
Young Pretender in 1745). During his time in
France, James studied mathematics and French
at the Brienne Military Academy; amongst his

fellow students was a young Corsican cadet, then still known as Napoleone Buonaparte.

When Magdalene's brother Basil, an officer in the Royal Navy, returned to England in 1817, he made two stops. On the first, in Madras, he took on board a passenger, Captain Henry Harvey. It wasn't unusual for army officers who needed to return home to hitch a lift in a naval ship – what was unusual was that this officer was to become Magdalene's second husband; and even more extraordinary, was that this was the second time Basil had been aboard the same ship - and become friends with - a man who would marry his sister: in 1808 he'd shared a cabin with William De Lancey. Unfortunately, Basil only discovered his sister had married De Lancey after his death. A final chance meeting occurred on Basil's second stop on the voyage home. Sir William De Lancey's brother-in-law, Sir Hudson Lowe, was now Governor of St Helena and so gaoler to the former Emperor Napoleon in his exile. On St Helena, Basil met Napoleon. The one time young Corsican cadet from Brienne told Basil that he remembered his father very well; Sir James, the former Emperor said, had been the first 'Englishman' he had ever met.

I am not the only person to find Magdalene's account remarkable. Charles Dickens, a friend of her brother Basil's, wrote to him to thank him for lending him the manuscript, saying, 'I shall never forget the lightest word of it... (I) never saw anything so real, so touching.' Walter Scott, another friend, wrote, 'certainly I would consider it as one of the most valuable and important documents which could be published as illustrative of the woes of war.'

I still find it extraordinary to feel a thread of connection to these momentous events. Magdalene's brother, Basil, was my great-great-great-grandfather on my mother's side, only three generations previous to my late grandfather who died in 2004. Grandpa remembered his own grandmother, Basil's daughter in law, Grace, who died in 1923. Suddenly the past doesn't seem remote at all.

I am proud of Magdalene, and of being related to her. She loses a man she loves unexpectedly and in the worst circumstances. She doesn't belittle her experience with a false stiff upper lip, but is always honest, 'I shall never get on if I begin to talk of what my happiness was; but I dread to enter on the gloomy past, which I shudder to look back upon, and I often wonder I survived it'. The story is coloured by her humility, her humanity and even, in the midst of the most awful horror, flashes of humour between her and her dying husband. She does all she can to save him pain and the poignancy of her trying to spare him the sight of her tears is almost too much: 'In an hour or two he ate some breakfast, tea and toasted bread, with so much relish that it almost overcame me. He observed that I must have caught cold by sitting in a draught of air. I said I had.' If I could write as beautifully as she did and love as well – and emulate some fraction of her generosity and nobility of spirit – I would feel I had lived a good life.

I would like to thank my uncle John, and my mother Marion for their encouragement and help in bringing my thoughts together. I would also like to thank my much missed late Grandpa, Douglas, and Granny Rachel; it was particularly Grandpa's -often tall- tales that made all of his grandchildren interested in family history. In addition, I would like to thank David Miller, whose *Lady De Lancey at Waterloo* is a mine of family information and was a great help to me in writing this preface.

London 2008

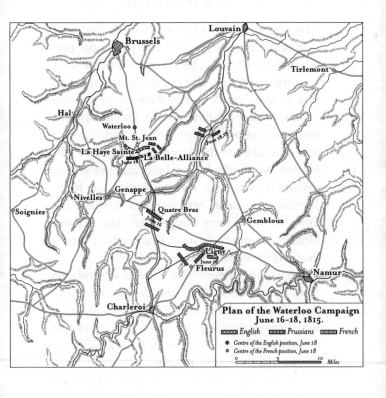

Plan of the Waterloo Campaign
June 16-18, 1815.

xxxxx *English*   xxxxx *Prussians*   ‖‖‖‖ *French*

● Centre of the English position, June 18
● Centre of the French position, June 18

0   5   10
Miles

Louvain

Brussels

Tirlemont

Hal

Waterloo
Mt. St. Jean
La Haye Sainte
June 18
La Belle-Alliance
June 18, 3

Genappe

Nivelles

Soignies

Quatre Bras
June 16

Gembloux

Ligny
June 16
Fleurus

Namur

Charleroi

"She was wrapped in a white morning dress, her hair falling on her shoulders, and her large eyes fixed and without light. By way of helping on the preparations for the departure, and showing that she too could be useful at a moment so critical, this poor soul had taken up a sash of George's from the drawers whereon it lay, and followed him to and fro with the sash in her hand, looking on mutely as his packing proceeded. She came out and stood, leaning at the wall, holding this sash against her bosom, from which the heavy net of crimson dropped like a large stain of blood. Our gentle-hearted Captain felt a guilty shock as he looked at her.

"Good God," thought he, "and is it grief like this I dared to pry into?" And there was no help: no means to soothe and comfort this helpless, speechless misery. He stood for a moment and looked at her, powerless and torn with pity, as a parent regards an infant in pain.

At last, George took Emmy's hand, and led her back into the bedroom, from whence he came out alone. The parting had taken place in that moment, and he was gone.

"Thank Heaven that is over," George thought, bounding down the stair, his sword under his arm, as he ran swiftly to the alarm-ground, where the regiment was mustered, and whither trooped men and officers hurrying from their billets, his pulse was throbbing and his cheeks flushed: the

great game of war was going to be played, and
he one of the players. What a fierce excitement
of doubt, hope, and pleasure! What tremendous
hazards of loss or gain! What were all the games
of chance he had ever played compared to this
one?"

Vanity Fair, William Makepeace Thackeray.

"The road was ankle-deep in mud and slough; and we had not proceeded a quarter of a mile when we heard the trampling of horses' feet, and on looking round perceived a large cavalcade of officers coming at full speed. In a moment we recognised the Duke himself at their head. He was accompanied by the Duke of Richmond, and his son, Lord William Lennox. The entire Staff of the army was close at hand: the Prince of Orange, Count Pozzo di Borgo, Baron Vincent, the Spanish General Alava, Prince Castel Cicala, with their several aides-de-camp; Felton Hervey, Fitzroy Somerset, and De Lancey were the last that appeared. They all seemed as gay and un-concerned as if they were riding to meet the hounds in some quiet English county."

Captain Rees Howell Gronow, a subaltern of the 1st Guards at Waterloo from *Recollections and Anecdotes*, by Captain Rees Howell Gronow, 1866.

LADY DE LANCEY
From a mignature after J.D. Engleheart

MAGDALENE DE LANCEY
A Week At Waterloo

I arrived at Brussels on Thursday, 8th June 1815, and was much surprised at the peaceful appearance of that town, and the whole country from Ostend. We were billeted in the house of the Count de Lannoy, in the Park, which is a square of very beautiful houses with fine large trees in the centre. The Count de Lannoy was very attentive, and we had a suite of very excellent rooms, up four stories, which is the fashion in that country, I believe. It was amusing enough, sometimes, to see from our windows the people parading in the Park. I saw very little of the town, and still less of the inhabitants; for notwithstanding Sir William's belief that we should remain quietly there for a month at least, I have the comfort of remembering that, as there was a chance we might separate in a few days, I wasted no time in visiting or going to balls, which I did not care for, and therefore I never went out, except for an hour or two every afternoon, to walk with Sir William.

The people in general dined between three

and four, we dined at six; we walked while others were at dinner, so that literally I never saw anybody, except some gentlemen, two or three of whom dined with us every day – Sir William's friends, whom he brought to introduce to me. I never passed such a delightful time, for there was always enough of very pleasant society to keep us gay and merry, and the rest of the day was spent in peaceful happiness.

Fortunately my husband had scarcely any business to do, and he only went to the office for about an hour every day. I then used to sit and think with astonishment of my being transported into such a scene of happiness, so perfect, so unalloyed! feeling that I was entirely enjoying life not a moment wasted. How active and how well I was! I scarcely knew what to do with all my health and spirits. Now and then a pang would cross my mind at the prospect of the approaching campaign, but I chased away the thought, resolved not to lose the present bliss by dwelling on the chance of future pain. Sir William promised to let me know as soon as he knew himself, everything concerning the movement of the army; and accordingly he gave me every paper to read, to keep my mind easy. After some consideration, he decided that upon the commencement of hostilities I should go to Antwerp, and there remain till the end of the campaign, which might last months. He wished me not to think of going along with him, because the rear of a great army was always dangerous, and an unfit situation for a woman; and he wished not to draw me into any scenes, or near any danger, more than if I had remained in England. He little thought I should be in the midst of horrors I would not pass again for any being now living; and alas, the cautious anxiety he expressed that I should avoid being shocked, only made me feel more desolate and miserable when I found myself in the midst of most terrible scenes.

Several other officers, on hearing that he designed to send me to Antwerp, fixed that their wives should go there too. It is a very strongly fortified town, and likewise having the sea to escape by, if necessary, it was by far the safest place; and being only twenty-five miles from Brussels, it added so little to the time of hearing from him, if separated, that I acquiesced cheerfully. After this was arranged, we never thought more about it, and enjoyed each hour as it passed with no more anxiety than was sufficient to render time precious.

On Wednesday the 14th, I had a little alarm in the evening with some public papers, and Sir William went out with them, but returned in a short time; and it passed by so completely, that Thursday forenoon was the happiest day of my life; but I cannot recollect a day of my short married life that was not perfect. I shall never get on if I begin to talk of what my happiness was; but I dread to enter on the gloomy past, which I shudder to look back upon, and I often wonder I survived it. We little dreamt that Thursday was the last we were to pass together, and that the storm would burst so soon. Sir William had to dine at the Spanish ambassador's - the first invitation he had accepted from the time I went; he was unwilling to go, and delayed and still delayed, till at last when near six, I fastened all his medals and crosses on his coat, helped him to put it on, and he went. I watched at the window till he was out of sight, and then I continued musing on my happy fate; I thought over all that had passed, and how grateful I felt! I had no wish but that this might continue; I saw my husband loved and respected by everyone, my life gliding on, like a gay dream, in his care.

When I had remained at the window nearly an hour, I saw an aide-de-camp ride under the gateway of our house. He sent to enquire where Sir William was dining. I wrote down the name; and soon after I saw him gallop off in that direction. I did not like this appearance, but I tried not to be afraid. A few minutes after, I saw Sir William on the same horse gallop past to the Duke's, which was a few doors beyond ours.[1] He dis-

---

[1] The De Lancey's were staying at the south-east corner of the Impasse du Parc and the Duke of Wellington at the corner of the Rue de la Montagne du Parc and the Rue Royale.

mounted and ran into the house - left the horse in the middle of the street. I must confess my courage failed me now, and the succeeding two hours formed a contrast to the happy forenoon.

About nine, Sir William came in; seeing my wretched face, he bade me not be foolish, for it would soon be all over now; they expected a great battle on the morrow; he would send me to Antwerp in the morning, and desired me to be ready at six. He said that though he expected it would be a decisive battle, and a conclusion of the whole business, he thought it best I should keep the plan of going to Antwerp, to avoid the alarms that he knew would seize everyone the moment the troops were gone; and he said he would probably join me there, or send for me to return the same evening. He said he should be writing all night, perhaps: he desired me to prepare some strong green tea in case he came in, as the violent exertion requisite to setting the whole army in motion quite stupefied him sometimes. He used sometimes to tell me that whenever the operations began, if he thought for five minutes on any other subject, he was neglecting his duty. I therefore scrupulously avoided asking him any questions, or indeed speaking at all. I moved up and down like one stupefied myself.

He went to the office, and returned near twelve, much fatigued, but he did not attempt to sleep; he went twice to the Duke's; the first time he found him standing looking over a map with a Prussian general, who was in full-dress uniform - with orders and crosses, etc. - the Duke was in his chemise and slippers, preparing to dress for the Duchess of Richmond's ball; the two figures were quite admirable. The ball took place notwithstanding the reveille played through the streets the whole night. Many of the officers danced, and then marched in the morning.[1]

About two, Sir William went again to the Duke, and he was sleeping sound! At three the troops were all assembled in the Park, and Sir William and I leant over the window, seeing them march off - so few to return. It was a clear refreshing morning, and the scene was very solemn and melancholy. The fifes played alone, and the regiments one after another marched past, and I saw them melt away through the great gate at the end of the Square. Shall I ever forget the tunes played by the shrill fifes and the buglehorns which disturbed that night!

At six in the morning, Friday the 16th, I went to Antwerp: Sir William gave me a letter to Captain Mitchell, in the Q.M.-General's department, requesting him to take charge of me.

Accordingly, soon after we arrived I was settled

---

[1] Magdalene De Lancey and her husband were amongst the guests invited to the Duchess of Richmond's famous ball but as she makes no reference to getting dressed to go it is fair to assume that they had no intention of going. Many of the officers who were killed in the battle that followed died in their shoes and silk stockings.

in very comfortable apartments. I was at first for an hour in the inn, and I lay down in a small back room. In the evening I sent my maid from the lodgings to get some wine at the inn; when wandering in the passage to find some English person, she opened the door of the room I had been in, and saw the body of the Duke of Brunswick on the very bed.

I was fortunate enough to have a room at the back, so shut in with buildings that I could not hear any noise in the streets. Sir William had made me promise to believe no reports, and not upon any account to move without his written order for it. I thought it was best not to listen to any stories, so I told my maid Emma not to tell me any, and to do her best to get no alarms herself. Captain Mitchell I found of great service; he is a very sensible and seemingly good-hearted man. There was a calmness in his manner which was of infinite use to me when I could not entirely get the better of fears but too well founded. Though he was afterwards oppressed with business, night and day, he never failed to come to me when he had heard any accounts he could depend upon. But I may say I never saw so much kindness, and softness indeed, as during that miserable time.

The general and individual distress that rapidly followed the battles then fought, seemed quite to unman them; and one grew accustomed to see men weep, without their attempting to conceal it. The same evening the Town Major, Machel, called. He knew Sir William, and he brought a Mrs – to call. She very kindly asked me to go and visit her in the country about a mile. I was much obliged to her, but said I hoped to return to Brussels so soon that I should not have time. She apologised for Mr –; he would have called on me, but the report I had brought of the marching of the troops had given him a great deal of business. The town was now very bustling, though when I arrived there was nothing but quiet. Captain Mitchell told me in the evening that the battle had taken place; that the English had gained a victory, but he believed there was to be more fighting. He promised to send me any letter, or if he heard of Sir William. I sat up late, but none came.

On Saturday the 17th, Antwerp was truly a scene of confusion – by the servant's account, for I would not stir out of my room. Not one of the ladies who had intended to come to Antwerp at first, kept their resolution; and in consequence they got a great alarm, which was what my husband wished me to escape. There was a battle fought on Friday the 16th, near Brussels, and I was told the noise of the cannon was so tremendous – the houses shook with it.[1] It was distinctly heard at Antwerp; but I kept the windows shut, and tried not to hear. I only heard a rolling like

the sea at a distance. Poor Emma, urged by curios-
ity, stood in the street listening to terrible stories,
seeing wounded men brought in, carriages full of
women and children flying from Brussels, till she
was completely frightened. She came and told
me that all the ladies were hastening to England
by sea, for the French had taken Brussels. I saw
I must take my time to alarm her, and I said,
"Well, Emma, you know that if the French were
firing at this house, I would not move till I was
ordered; but you have no such duty, therefore go
if you like. I dare say any of the families will let
you join them."

Emma was shocked at my supposing she
would be so base as to desert me, and declared
that if she was sure she had to remain in a French
prison for five years, she would not leave me.
My reproof had all the effect I intended; for she
brought me no more stories, and I am certain she
never was frightened after, even when we were
in far greater danger.

Though I had little reason to expect a letter
from my husband, I sat up late in hopes. At mid-
night, what was my joy to get a little note from
him, written at Genappe, after the battle of the
16th.[2] He said he was safe, and in great spirits;

---

[1] These were in fact the two battles of Ligny and Quatre Bras,
which were not fought anywhere near Brussels; but in Antwerp,
Magdalene De Lancey could not have known that.

[2] The Duke of Wellington dined at the Roi d'Espagne in Genappe
prior to setting up his HQ at Waterloo.

they had given the French a tremendous beating.
I wrote to him every day, and Captain Mitchell
sent my letters, but they never reached him.

On Sunday, Captain Mitchell told me he had
heard the last effort was to be made. I cannot
attempt to describe the restless unhappy state
I was in; for it had continued so much longer
than I had expected already, that I began to find
it difficult to keep up my spirits, though I was
infatuated enough to think it quite impossible
that he could be hurt. I believe mine was not
an uncommon case, but so it was. I might be
uneasy at the length of the separation, or anxious
to hear from him; but the possibility of his being
wounded never glanced into my mind, till I was
told he was killed.

On Sunday the 18th June, there was to be a
great battle. It began about eleven; near three,
when Sir William was riding beside the Duke, a
cannon ball struck him on the back, at the right
shoulder, and knocked him off his horse to several yards distance. The Duke at first imagined he
was killed; for he said afterwards, he had never in
all the fighting he had ever been in seen a man
rise again after such a wound. Seeing he was alive
(for he bounded up again and then sank down),
he ran to him, and stooping down, took him by
the hand.

Sir William begged the Duke, as the last favour he could have it in his power to do him,

to exert his authority to take away the crowd that gathered round him, and to let him have his last moments in peace to himself. The Duke bade him farewell, and endeavoured to draw away the Staff, who oppressed him; they wanted to take leave of him, and wondered at his calmness. He was left, as they imagined, to die; but his cousin, Delancey Barclay, who had seen him fall, went to him instantly, and tried to prevail upon him to be removed to the rear, as he was in imminent danger of being crushed by the artillery, which was fast approaching the spot; and also there was danger of his falling into the hands of the enemy. He entreated to be left on the ground, and said it was impossible he could live; that they might be of more use to others, and he only begged to remain on the field. But as he spoke with ease, and Colonel Barclay saw that the ball had not entered, he insisted on moving him, and he took the opinion of a surgeon, who thought he might live, and got some soldiers to carry him in a blanket to a barn at the side of the road, a little to the rear. The wound was dressed, and then Colonel Barclay had to return to the Division; but first he gave orders to have Sir William moved to the village; for that barn was in danger of being taken possession of by the enemy. Before Colonel Barclay went, Sir William begged him to come quite close to him, and continued to give him messages for me. Nothing else seemed to occupy his mind. He desired him to write to me at Antwerp; to say everything kind, and to endeavour to soften this business, and to break it to me as gently as he could. He then said he might move him, as if he fancied it was to be his last effort. He was carried to the village of Waterloo, and left in a cottage, where he lay unheeded all night, and part of next day. Many of his friends were in the village, and no one knew where he was, or that he was alive even. It was by chance that an officer of the Staff Corps found him next morning, and sent to inform Sir George Scovell. The evening before, the Duke had written the despatches, and had inserted De Lancey as killed. Interest was made that he should alter them, when he was told that he had been carried off the field alive. Some kindly thought this might benefit me; but I was not so fortunate. Sad scenes were passing at Antwerp in the meantime.

On Monday morning, Captain Mitchell, at nine o'clock, came to tell me that the last battle was over, and the French entirely defeated, and that Sir William was safe. I asked him repeatedly if he was sure, and if he had seen any of his writing, or if he had heard from him. He had not; but had read a list of the killed and wounded, and could assure me his name was not in it. Captain Mitchell was quite sincere; and was afterwards much grieved that he had added to the accumulation of misery, for this only made the dash down more severe. I now found how much I had really feared by the wild spirits I got into. I walked up and down, for I could not rest, and was almost in a fever with happiness, and for two hours this went on.

At eleven a message came that Lady Hamilton wished to see me. I went down to the parlour, and found her and Mr James. I did not remark anything in her countenance, but I think I never saw feeling and compassion more strongly marked than in his expression. I then said I hoped Lady Emily was well. He answered that she was so, with a tone of such misery that I was afraid something had happened, I knew not what, to somebody. I looked at Lady Hamilton for an explanation. She seemed a little agitated too, and I said, "One is so selfish: I can attend to nothing, I am so rejoiced Sir William is safe."

Mr James walked to the other end of the room. I did not know what to do. I feared that my gay voice grieved them, for I saw something had made them unhappy. Little did I think the blow was falling on my own unfortunate head.

Lady Hamilton said, "Poor Mr James! He has lost a brother and I a nephew. It was a dreadful battle! – so many killed."

I thought it cruel of them to come to me to tell all this to, when I was so merry; but I tried to be polite, and again apologised for appearing glad, on account of my own good fortune.

Lady Hamilton said, "Did you hear from him?"

"No, but Captain Mitchell saw the list, and his name was not in it."

Mr James went out of the room. Lady Hamilton said, "He is gone to see it, I suppose," and then began to talk about the list, and what were the first names, and a great deal about whether I had any friends in that country, etc. She then asked what I intended to do if the fighting continued, and if I should go to England? I was a little surprised at these enquiries, but assured her I would not move until Sir William came or sent for me. She found me so obstinately confident that she began... - and after a short time a suspicion darted into my mind. What a death-like feeling was that!

Lady Hamilton confessed she had written the list, and with a most mistaken kindness had omitted several of the names, Sir William's among the rest. A general had come from the field and named them; and she, knowing I was in the country, had left his out, fearing that I should be suddenly informed. But such information would not be otherwise than a shock whatever way it was told, and the previous account of his safety only tortured me the more. But it is needless to dwell upon it now; and though I believe she thinks I never forgave her, now recollect only the motive, which was kind.

My difficulty then was to find out, or rather

to believe the truth. She assured me he was only wounded. I looked at her keenly, and said, "Lady Hamilton, I can bear anything but suspense. Let me know the very worst. Tell me, is he killed?"

She then solemnly assured me he was only desperately wounded.

I shook my head and said, "Ah, it is very well to say so. Yes, he must be wounded first, you know." And I walked round the room fast.

"Yes, yes, you say so, but I cannot believe what you say now."

She was terrified, for I could not shed a tear. She declared upon her word of honour that when General Alava left the field he was alive, but was not expected to live. This I felt sounded like truth, and I stood before her and said, "Well, Lady Hamilton, if it is so, and you really wish to serve me, help me to go to him instantly. I am sure Mr James will be so good as to hurry the servant. Oh, how much time has been lost already! If Captain Mitchell had but known, I should have gone at nine. Every moment may make me too late to see him alive."

She was glad to try to do anything for me, and was going. I stopped her at the door, and said, "Now, if you are deceiving me, you may perhaps have my senses to answer for."

She repeated her assurances, and I said I would send my servant for the carriage, which was at the Town Major's, if she would see anybody to get horses, and I was ready. She said she would offer to go with me, but she knew it would oppress me.

I said, "Oh no, let me be alone," and I ran upstairs.

No power can describe my sufferings for two hours before I could set out. Captain Mitchell requested a friend of his to ride forward to Brussels, and to gallop back with information of where Sir William was, and whether it was still of any avail for me to proceed: he was expected to meet us at Malines, half-way. We at last left Antwerp; but bribing the driver was in vain. It was not in his power to proceed; for the moment we passed the gates, we were entangled in a crowd of waggons, carts, horses, wounded men, deserters or runaways, and all the rabble and confusion, the consequence of several battles. Every now and then we went several miles at a walk; and the temper of the people was so irritable that we feared to speak to them; and I had to caution my servant to be very guarded, because they were ready to draw their swords in a moment. Two men got on the back of the carriage, and we dared not desire them to get off; and this was no imaginary terror, as I afterwards experienced.

When we were within a mile or two of Malines, the carriage stopped, and the servant said, "It is the Captain." I had drawn the blinds to avoid seeing the wretched objects we were pass-

ing. I hastily looked out, and saw Mr Hay. When
he saw me he turned his head away.

I called out, "Mr Hay, do you know anything?"

He hesitated, and then said, "I fear I have very
bad news for you."

I said, "Tell me at once. Is he dead?"

"It is all over."

I sank into the carriage again, and they took
me back to Antwerp. When I had been a short
time there, Mr Hay sent to know if I had any
commands to Brussels, as he was going to return,
and would do anything for me there. At first I
said I had none, and then I sent for him, and
asked repeatedly if he were sure of what he said;
if he had seen him fall. He had not been in the
action, and of course was not near Sir William,
"who was surrounded by Lord Wellington's Staff;
but in the middle of the action he was struck in
the breast by a cannon ball, and instantly fell.

The Duke went and leant over him, and he
died like a soldier."

I then begged Mr Hay to make a point of
seeing someone who had been near him; and
if possible to learn if he had spoken, and if he
had named me. Mr Hay promised this, and then
asked if I would choose to go to England. I said:
"Instantly." He then said if he had twelve hours
to search the field once more - for his brother
was missing - he would be ready to take a passage

for me, and to accompany me if I chose. He said Lady Hamilton and Mrs B. were below, anxious to be of use.

I said I greatly preferred being alone, and was always much better alone. About half an hour after, Mrs B. contrived to get into the room. I was terrified, and called out, "Go away, go away, leave me to myself." She prayed and entreated me to hear her, and then said if I was ill would I send for her. I said, "Oh, yes, yes; but the only thing anybody can do for me is to leave me alone." She was alarmed at my violent agitation and went away. I locked the outer door, and shut the inner one, so that no one could again intrude. They sent Emma to entreat I would be bled; but I was not reasonable enough for that, and would not comply. I wandered about the room incessantly, beseeching for mercy, though I felt that now, even Heaven could not be merciful. One is apt to fix on a situation just a little less wretched than one's own, and to dwell upon the idea that one could bear that better. I repeated over and over that if I had seen him alive for five minutes, I would not repine. At night Emma brought her bed into my room, as she feared I should be ill. Towards morning I fancied I heard a sound of someone trying to get into the room. I heard it a long while, but thinking it was somebody coming to visit me, I made no answer.

About two hours after, the attempt was repeated. I said to Emma, "There is a noise at the door. Don't let Mrs B. in, or Lady Hamilton."

She went, and returning in a few minutes said, "I am desired to tell you cautiously."

I said, "Oh Emma! Go away. Don't tell me anything, any more."

"Nay, but I must tell you. I have good news for you."

"How can you be so inhuman! What is good news for me now?"

"But – Sir William is not dead."

I started up, and asked what she was saying, for she would make me mad. She told me that General M'Kenzie was below, and had a message from Brussels, requesting him to inform me that Sir William was alive, and that there were even hopes of his recovery.

I ran down to General M'Kenzie, and began earnestly to persuade him it must be impossible. I had suffered so much the day before, I durst not hope for anything now. His voice faltered, and his eyes filled with tears.

He said, "Can you believe any man would bring such intelligence unless it were well- founded?" He then gave me a letter from Sir G. Scovell, who had seen an officer of the Staff Corps who had seen Sir William alive that morning, who was anxious to see me. He was attended by a skilful surgeon, and had been twice bled. This was dated Monday, seven o'clock, evening.

I regretted the deal of time that had been lost, and said that yesterday morning was a long time ago; and was no argument for his being alive now; for it was often repeated in the letter not to raise my hopes. I then asked General M'Kenzie to assist me to get away.

Unfortunately I did not say I had a carriage. He said he was going to Brussels, and would take me. I consented, and he went to get ready. I would not if I could, describe the state I was in for two hours more; then I lost all self-command. I would not allow Emma to put up my clothes, for fear of being detained. My agitation and anxiety increased. I had the dreadful idea haunting me that I should arrive perhaps half an hour too late. This got the better of me, and I paced backward and forward in the parlour very fast, and my breathing was like screaming. I went into the passage, and sent Emma to see if the carriage were coming; and then sat down on the stair, which was steep and dark. There General M'Kenzie found me. Whenever he learnt I had a carriage, he sent the horses he had; for his carriage was not ready, and would not be for some time. When he saw what a state I was in, he roused me in a most sensible manner.

He said, "Lady De Lancey, consider what you are doing. You are exhausting your strength and spirits to no purpose, for your friends are endeavouring to forward your departure as soon as possible."

I exclaimed, "Oh, I shall never be there. He may be dying at this moment."

He took my hand, and said calmly and firmly, "My dear madam, why fancy evil? You know what dreadful scenes you may have to go through when you reach Waterloo. You will probably require all your courage, and must command yourself for his sake."

I said no more, but quietly went to the parlour and remained waiting – such an immediate effect had his steady good sense on my fevered mind. I overheard him say, "No, do not at present; she is not fit for it." I was alarmed, and ran out; but I saw a lady retreating, and I was grateful to him.

We left Antwerp between eight and nine, and had the same difficulties to encounter; but the road was not quite so much blocked up. General M'Kenzie said he would ride after us in an hour, in case we should be detained; he also sent a dragoon before, to order horses. When we were near Vilvorde, the driver attempted to pass a waggon, but the soldier who rode beside it would not move one inch to let us pass. The wagons kept possession of the *chaussée* the whole way, and we had to drive on the heavy road at the side. My servant got off the seat to endeavour to lead the horses past. This provoked the soldier, and a dispute began. I was alarmed, and desired the servant to get upon the carriage again, which he

did. A Prussian officer, enraged at our attempting to pass the waggon he was guarding, drew
his sword, and made several cuts at the servant's
legs, but did not reach him. He was preparing to
get down again, but I looked from the opposite
window and commanded him to sit still, and not
to answer a word; or else to quit the carriage
altogether. The driver now made a dash past the
waggon, and the officer galloped after us and
attempted to wound the horses. This made me
desperate, and I ventured on a most imprudent
action. I drew up the blind, and holding up my
hands, I petitioned him to let us pass. I exclaimed
that my husband, a British officer, was dying, and
if he detained me I might not see him. It had
the desired effect, for without seeming to have
heard me, he slackened his pace and was soon
far behind.

When within ten miles of Brussels, the smell
of gunpowder was very perceptible. The heat was
oppressive. As we came within a mile of Brussels,
the multitude of wretched - looking people was
great, as Emma told me, for I was both unwilling
and unable to look out. I was so much worn with
anxiety that I could scarcely sit up. As we entered
Brussels the carriage stopped, and I saw Mr Hay.
I durst not speak, but he instantly said, "He is
alive. I sent my servant to Waterloo this morning;
he is just returned, and Sir William is better than
they expected. I have horses standing harnessed,

and you will soon be there if the road is passable, though it was not yesterday, for a horse."

We were soon out of Brussels again, and on the road to Waterloo. It is nine miles, and we took three hours and a half. Mr Hay rode before us with his sword drawn, and obliged them to let us pass. We often stood still for ten minutes. The horses screamed at the smell of corruption, which in many places was offensive. At last, when near the village, Mr Hay said he would ride forward and find the house, and learn whether I should still proceed or not. I hope no one will ever be able to say they can understand what my feelings must have been during the half-hour that passed till he returned. How fervently and sincerely I resolved that if I saw him alive for one hour I never would repine! I had almost lost my recollection, with the excess of anxiety and suspense, when Mr Hay called out, "All's well; I have seen him. He expects you."

When we got to the village, Sir G. Scovell met the carriage, and opening the door, said, "Stop one moment."

I said, "Is he alive?"

"Yes, alive; and the surgeons are of opinion that he may recover. We are so grieved for what you have suffered."

"Oh! never mind what I have suffered. Let me go to him now."

He said I must wait one moment. I assured

him I was composed indeed.

He said, "I see you are," with a smile," but I wish to warn you of one thing. You must be aware that his life hangs on a very slender hold; and therefore any agitation would be injurious. Now, we have not told him you had heard of his death; we thought it would afflict him; therefore do not appear to have heard it."

I promised, and he said, "Now come along." I sat down for an instant in the outer room, and he went in; and when I heard my husband say, "Let her come in, then," I was overpaid for all the misery.

I was surprised at the strength of his voice, for I had expected to find him weak and dying.

When I went into the room where he lay, he held out his hand and said, " Come, Magdalene, this is a sad business, is it not?" I could not speak, but sat down by him and took his hand. This was my occupation for six days.

Though I found him far better than I expected, I can scarcely say whether I hoped or feared most at first; because I was so much occupied with gathering comforts about him, and helping him, that I had not time to think about the future. It was a dreadful but sufficient preparation, being told of his death; and then finding him alive, I was ready to bear whatever might ensue without a murmur. I was so grateful for seeing him once more, that I valued each hour as it passed, and as I had too much reason to fear that I should very soon have nothing left of happiness but what my reflections would afford me, I endeavoured, by suppressing feelings that would have made him miserable, and myself unfit to serve him, to lay up no store of regret. He asked me if I was a good nurse. I told him that I had not been much tried.

He said he was sure he would be a good patient, for he would do whatever I bade him till he was convalescent; and then he knew he would grow very cross. I watched in vain for a cross word. All his endeavour seemed to be to leave none but pleasing impressions on my mind; and as he grew worse and suffered more, his smile was more sweet, and his thanks more fervent, for everything that was done for him.

I endeavoured to find out from the surgeons the extent of the danger. They said that at present there were no bad symptoms, and after seeing him alive at all after such a wound they would not despair: and if the fever could be kept off, there was a great chance of his recovering. With this view they wished to bleed him constantly; wishing also thereby to make the recovery more complete. I knew they had no interest in me, and therefore would probably tell me the same as other people, so I continued to ask them after every visit what they thought; but when by watching the symptoms myself and also observ-

ing the surgeon's expression, I saw what I must
soon prepare for. I did not tease them any more
with questions, but tried not to give way, and
endeavoured to keep up as long as it would be
of consequence to him; for even after all hope
was gone and the disorder increased rapidly, I felt
that if by agitating him I should afterwards im-
agine I had shortened his life by one hour, that
reflection would embitter my whole life. I have
the satisfaction of knowing that I succeeded even
better than I could have hoped; for toward the
end of the week, when every symptom was bad,
the surgeon (probably because I desisted from
enquiring and did not appear agitated) doubtful
what I thought, yet, judging it right to tell me,
asked Emma if she knew whether I was aware of
the danger or not. She assured him I had entirely
given up hope for some time.

I found Emma of great service. Her good will
carried her through excessive fatigue while at
Waterloo; and afterwards her excellent heart and
superior judgment were quite a blessing to me.
She told me she was thankful she had been at
Waterloo, for it would do her good to see a little
of what other people endured. She never before
knew half the value of her peaceful, comfortable
home in London, where the absence of miserable
objects might alone be considered as a benefit. I
can hardly express what I felt on returning to
England, to see people surrounded with every

luxury unhappy at the want of the smallest comfort. I can fancy no better cure for all imaginary
evils than a week's residence at Waterloo.

Noise did not disturb Sir William, fortunately,
for the cottage was surrounded with roads. One
in front led to Nivelles, and every waggon going
to and from the army, and all the wounded and
prisoners, passed along that road. It was paved,
and there was an unceasing noise for four days
and nights. We were obliged to keep the windows open, and people used to pass close to that
in his room, talking loud, and sometimes looking
in and speaking; but he never took any notice.
I never saw anybody so patient. The people to
whom the cottage belonged were, luckily, favour-
able to our cause, or they would have tormented
us a good deal; instead of which, I never met
with such good nature; and though they never
rested one moment helping the soldiers to water, and were constantly worn out with giving
them assistance, we had only to tell them what
to do, and they ran about to work for us. Their
ménage, I must allow, was in a sad state. There was
a want of everything. I could not help thinking with envy of the troublesome abundance I
had often seen in sick-rooms, when there was far
less need for it. However, in a short time we got
everything he required; and I have the greatest
comfort in recollecting that there was not one
thing which he expressed a wish for that we did

not procure. I sent a servant instantly to Brussels with a list of things we wanted; and once I recollect something was brought which he had been very anxious for. Naturally enough, he was disappointed when he found it not so good as he expected; but I was quite struck with his endeavour to praise it, for fear I should be sorry. There was a languid melancholy about him at the same time that he was calm and resigned, which would have made the most uninterested person grieved to see him suffering, and with such sweetness. Emma once gave him some drink, and she told me that the tone of voice and his smile when he thanked her, was like to break her heart, for he was in severe pain at the time.

He said the wound gave him no pain at all, but a little irritating cough caused excessive pain in his chest and side. As far as I could learn, the blow had affected the lungs, which produced inflammation and afterwards water in the chest, which was eventually the cause of his death. I suspect the surgeons had never much hope, but they said there was a chance if the inflammation could have been stopped. By constantly watching him, and gradually day after day observing the progress and increase of suffering and the elevated tone of his mind, along with fatigue and weakness, I was prepared for his final release in a manner that nothing but his firmness and composure could have effected.

He had at first been laid in the outer room, which had two large windows to the road, and everyone saw in. This he did not like, and he made the people move him to a small room, about seven feet wide, with a bed across the end of it. They placed him so low and awkwardly in the bed, that when I first went in I thought his legs were hurt, for he could not straighten his knees. After a day or two, he got shoved up by degrees, and then could stretch his limbs. The bed was wretched, merely a wooden frame fastened to the wall, so that it could not be moved, which rendered it extremely difficult to bleed him, or to assist him in any way, as he could neither turn nor raise his head an inch from the pillow, or rather sack of chaff, upon which he was laid. This was so full of dust that it made him cough. I soon removed it, and got a cushion out of the carriage instead. We had a clean blanket from Brussels, and at first we put clean sheets on every day. But latterly he grew so restless that he preferred having only the blanket. I had purposely sent for a French cotton one, as I thought the flannel would tease him. The bed was made tolerable at least, and though I could not be pleased with it, he was. He repeated more than once, "What a thing it was for you being in this country!" and I had the delight of hearing him say that he did not know what he would have done without me. He said he was sure he would not have lived so long, for he would not have been so obedient to anyone else.

I found he had been the worse of seeing some friends who had called the first day I was at Waterloo, so I told the servant afterwards never to let anybody come into his room. I remember one day an officer called, and before he was out of sight I had his card converted into a teaspoon. Sir William never ate anything, except once or twice a morsel of toast out of the water. He drank a great deal of tea and lemonade. At first he had no milk to his tea, and he complained that it was very bad; but there was none to be got. I sent my servant to search for some, and he met some Prussian cows, and milked one, and brought a fine jug of milk.

The different contrivances sometimes amused him. One day he wished to have the room fumigated. How was this to be done, without fire-irons, or indeed without fire? We put some vinegar into a tumbler, and Emma went with a large pair of scissors, and brought a piece of burning charcoal, and put it into the vinegar, and that made a great smoke. Every time we wanted anything warmed, or water boiled, Emma had to cross a court and make a fire, and then watch it, or someone would have run away with what she was cooking. Meantime I would call her ten different times, and this in wet or dry, night or day. I now regretted having brought so few clothes.

The day I went to Waterloo, Sir William told me the Duke had visited him in the morning. He said he never had seen him so warm in his feelings: he had taken leave of him with little hope of seeing him again, I fancy. The Duke told him he never wished to see another battle; this had been so shocking. It had been too much to see such brave men, so equally matched, cutting each other to pieces as they did. Sir William said there never had been such fighting; that the Duke far surpassed anything he had ever done before. The general opinion seemed to be that it had been a peculiarly shocking battle. Sir William said he never would try it again; he was quite tired of the business. In speaking of his wound he said this might be the most fortunate event that could have happened for us both. I looked at him for an explanation. He said, "Certainly, even if I recover completely, I should never think of serving again. Nobody could ask such a thing, and we should settle down quietly at home for the rest of our lives."

The evening after I went to Waterloo, Sir G. Scovell said he would take something to eat, and after seeing me fairly established he would go to Headquarters. He wrote a copy of a return of rations, for which we were to send to Brussels; and also any other provisions must be got from thence, for the village produced nothing. He left two sentinels, for fear there should be any disturbances, and we might feel unprotected. One night there was a great noise of people quarrelling in front of the house; the windows had no fastening whatever, but they passed away without molesting us. I was a little more seriously alarmed another day. Some reports had reached us that the French were coming back, and were within nine miles. I thought it unlikely, but about eight in the morning all the waggons that had passed for two hours came back as fast as possible, horses trotting and men running. I was uneasy on Sir William's account: his situation was so helpless. I leant forward, to prevent people looking in and seeing him. I waited without saying anything, to learn the cause of this bustle. I found afterwards that it was merely the waggons had gone several miles on the wrong road, and were hurrying back to make it up.

From the time Sir G. Scovell left us, we scarcely saw anybody but the surgeons. It must add very much to the fatigue of their business, having to do everything for the wounded whom they attend. Mr Powell, who attended most constantly to Sir William, and with evidently great anxiety for his recovery, was sometimes quite knocked up with walking many miles on the heavy road to the field and the cottages. He had some difficulty to consider me as a useful person. At first he used to ask me to tell the servant to come; but he learnt to employ me very soon.

The night I went, Sir William desired me to take some rest, for I looked ill. A portmanteau bed had been brought for me from Brussels. I left him reluctantly, for I grudged wasting any of such precious time, but he would not hear of my sitting up. I had just lain down with my clothes on - for there was no blanket, and the floor was damp tiles. I heard him call to his servant, who slept at the end of his room on a mattress. I jumped up and went to him, and did not leave him again. He wanted some drink, which I gave him, and then sat down beside him. He slept and woke every halfhour. He was not restless, nor had he any pain, but he was constantly thirsty.

On Wednesday he wished to have leeches applied to his side, where the bruise appeared. Mr Powell had no objection, and desired me to send for him when the leeches were brought from Brussels. I did so; but in the meantime, not knowing why he was sent for, I began as a matter of course to apply them. When he came, he apologised, and thanked me. I was not at first aware of how I was obliging him. He said he was very tired, and when he attempted to fix the leeches, he did not do it so well as I did. Next time they were to be applied, I asked if I should send for him. He said I was as good at it as any hospital nurse could be, and as he had scarcely had an hour's rest any night since the battle, he would be greatly obliged to me if I would take the trouble. Sir William alleged that I grew quite vain of my skill in tormenting my poor husband with these animals. The same day Dr Hume called in passing to Brussels, for ten minutes. I was a little provoked at the gaiety of his manner; the gravity he assumed at Brussels would have been suitable to the present scene. Though Sir William never complained, he was serious, and seemed inclined to be quiet, and neither to speak much nor to listen. He generally lay thinking, often conversed with me, but seemed oppressed with general conversation, and would not listen when anyone told him of the progress of the army. His thoughts were in a very different train. Dr Hume's rapid, lively visit annoyed me much.

I did not feel the effects of having sat up on Tuesday night till next night, but was resolved to fight against it. Sir William desired me to go to rest, as he had done the night before; but I only remained away till I had an excuse to return, and he always forgot a second time to bid me go. This was the only night I had real difficulty to keep awake; the noise of the carts assisted me a little. I counted the rushes of the chair, for want of occupation. Some people said, why did I not let my maid sit up; but that showed they did not understand; for if twenty people had sat up, it would have made no difference to me. I frequently rejoiced that I had no friend there who could exert authority to make me take care of myself, when my only wish was to keep up as long as he needed me.

On Thursday he was not quite so well. Before this he had been making a gradual progress, and he could move about with more ease. He spoke much better than he did at first. His countenance was animated; but I fear this was the beginning of the most dangerous symptoms, and I saw that the surgeon now became uneasy at the appearance of the blood; and Mr Woolriche, a very eminent surgeon, now constantly attended. He had come over once or twice before. General Dundas called this forenoon. He stayed only a minute, as Sir William was not so well, and I was busy. After he was away, I recollected having neglected to ask him to send a blanket and some wine. I never had time to eat, and I always forgot to get wine – as I could take a glass of that and a bit of bread in a moment – and my strength was failing. I looked out and saw him still at the door. I went out, and there were a number of people, Sir H. D. Hamilton, etc. I told General Dundas I had no blanket. "Bless me!" everyone exclaimed, "no blanket!" I said it was not of much consequence, as I never lay down, but the floor was so damp I was afraid my maid would be ill, and her help was very essential. I then asked for wine, both of which General Dundas sent down next day.

That night I had no difficulty in keeping awake. Sir William was restless and uncomfortable; his breathing was oppressed, and I had constantly to raise him on the pillow. The pain in his chest increased, and he was twice bled before morning. He was very much better on Friday forenoon. Mr Woolriche told us that every day since the battle the people of Brussels sent down carriages to take the wounded to the hospital; from twenty to thirty private carriages came every day.

On Friday evening Sir William was very feverish, and the appearance of the blood was very inflammatory. I had learnt now to judge for myself, as Mr Powell, seeing how anxious I was, sometimes had the kindness to give me a little instruction. About ten at night Mr Powell and Mr Woolriche came. "While I told them how Sir William had been since their last visit, and mentioned several circumstances that had occurred, I watched them and saw they looked at each other. I guessed their thoughts. I turned away to the window and wept.

They remained a little time, and I recovered myself enough to speak to them cheerfully as they went out. They lingered, and seemed to wish to speak to me, but I was well aware of what they had to say. I felt unable to hear it then, and I shut the door instead of going out. It was that night Mr Powell asked Emma if she knew what I thought. He desired to be sent for on the first appearance of change. At one in the morning he was in great pain, and as I raised him that he might breathe more freely, he looked so fixed that I was afraid he was just expiring. His arms were round my neck to raise himself by, and I thought we should both have been killed by the exertion. He asked if Mr Powell had not talked of bleeding him again. I said I had sent for him. He bled him then for the last time. From that moment all the fever was gone. Mr Powell said it was of consequence to keep him quiet, and if he would sleep calmly it would do him good.

At four in the morning I was called out to see a surgeon sent from Mr Powell, who was ill in bed. He came to know how Sir William was. He had slept a little till three; but the oppression was returning. This surgeon told me he had been anxious to speak to me several times, to tell me that it was he who had first seen him on the field, and who had given it as his opinion that he might live. He was grieved indeed to think that it should fall to his lot to tell me that it was the opinion of the surgeons that if I had anything particular to say to Sir William, I should not de-lay long.

I asked, "How long ? " He said they could not exactly tell.

I said, "Days or hours?"

He answered that the present symptoms would certainly not prove fatal within twelve hours. I left him, and went softly into my husband's room, for he was sleeping. I sat down at the other end

of the room, and continued looking at him, quite
stupefied; I could scarcely see. My mouth was so
parched that when I touched it, it felt as dry as
the back of my hand. I thought I was to die first.
I then thought, what would he do for want of
me during the remaining few hours he had to
live. This idea roused me, and I began to recollect
our helpless situation whatever happened, and
tried to think who I could inform of the circumstances. I was not long in deciding on General
Dundas, if he could be found, and have time to
come and take care of us both. I immediately
wrote a long letter to him, telling him how I was
situated, and begging that he would come after
twelve hours. I said I hoped I should be calm
and fit to act for myself; but as I had never been
near such a scene before, I knew not what effect it might have upon me. I therefore explained
what I wished might be done after all was over,
with respect to everything. I then sent the servant with the letter and orders to find General
Dundas, if he were within ten miles of Brussels.
A few hours after, I had one line from him to say
he would be at Waterloo in the evening.

After I had sent the letter, I sat down to consider what I was to do next. Though Sir William
was aware of his danger, I thought it my duty to
tell him how immediate the surgeons seemed to
think it. I knew he was far above being the worse
of such a communication, and I wished to know

if he had anything to say. I sat thinking about it, when he awoke and held out his hand for me to take my usual station by his bedside. I went and told him. We talked some time on the subject. He was not agitated, but his voice faltered a little, and he said it was sudden. This was the first day he felt well enough to begin to hope he should recover! He breathed freely, and was entirely free from pain; and he said he had been thinking if he could be removed to Brussels, he should get well soon.

I then asked if he had anything to desire me to do, or anything to say to anyone. He reminded me of what he had told me had engrossed his thoughts when he imagined himself dying on the field. He said he felt exactly the same now. He felt at peace with all the world; he knew he was going to a better one, etc., etc. He repeated most of what he had told me were his feelings before that – he had no sorrow but to part from his wife, no regret but leaving her in misery.

He seemed fatigued; and shutting his eyes, he desired me not to speak for a little. I then determined not to introduce the subject again, nor to speak about it unless he seemed to wish it, as I had done all that was necessary.

In an hour or two he ate some breakfast, tea and toasted bread, with so much relish that it almost overcame me. He observed that I must have caught cold by sitting in a draught of air. I said I

had. He felt so much better that I was anxious the
surgeon should see him. He came in the evening.
He was pleased to see Sir William free from pain,
but said there was scarcely a possibility of its con-
tinuing so. He said he might linger a day or two,
but that every symptom was bad. He advised me
to keep him as quiet and composed as possible. I
assured him no person had been in the room but
the surgeons whom he had brought to consult;
and I had sat beside him the whole day, scarcely
speaking. I said I had told Sir William his opinion
of his case. He said it had evidently not agitated
him, for his pulse was quite calm. Mr Woolriche
called in the afternoon; he was going to Brussels,
and would do anything there we wished. We had
nothing for him to do, and he was going when
he repeated the question. Sir William looked at
me earnestly, and said, "Magdalene, love, General
Dundas." I answered, "I wrote to him this morning," and nothing more passed.

Late in the evening, when we were as calm
and composed as could be, and I was sitting and
looking at him, and holding his hand as usual, Mr
Powell and Dr Hume came. He was even more
cheerful than before, paid a rapid, noisy visit, and
away again. It disturbed our tranquillity not a little, but he is reckoned so skilful that we ought to
have been glad to see him. He bade Sir William
rouse up, felt his pulse, and said it would bear
another bleeding yet, if necessary.

The poor dying man raised his languid eyes, and said, "Oh no, I do not need it now; I am quite cool."

Dr Hume said he had no wish to bleed him, but would like to have his limbs fomented. He shook his head. I asked him if he knew what it was. He said No, and would like to try. I asked Dr Hume if it would be advisable. He said he thought it might refresh him. He went out, and I followed to hear what he would say. He said to Mr Powell, "Why do you give up a man with such a pulse? with such a good constitution, too! You make them all sad and useless. It does no harm to be trying something."

He named several things. "Put a blister on his breast, and leeches after, if the pain is great down the side."

I looked at Mr Powell, doubting, as I depended most on his opinion, as his constant attention to the progress of the illness gave it most weight. I thought he looked sorry that my hopes should be renewed, but of course he said nothing.

Dr Hume said, "Oh, don't fear, he won't desert the cause."

I was angry at such nonsense, and said, "Be assured I do not fear that Mr Powell will desert us, but he said this morning there was no hope."

"Nay," said he, "not quite so much as that: I said there was little hope."

I went away, and left them to discuss it themselves.

Sir William said he wished to try what Dr Hume was speaking of, and I went to order some boiling water to be prepared. I made the people understand that he wanted a great quantity in a tub. While I was speaking, Mr Powell returned. He had taken a turn with Dr Hume, and I fancy he had explained his opinion. He said he would go home and prepare a blister, and he believed we had leeches.

I said, was it not a great pity to torment him. He said he would not pretend to say that he thought it could be of much consequence, but for this reason he advised me to do it: I was not aware, he said, how I should feel afterwards; and I might perhaps regret when it was too late, not having done everything which a physician of Dr Hume's eminence deemed advisable. He said that Sir William would not be at ease at any rate, and it would scarcely plague him; the fomentation would be pleasant to him, and I might take the blister off in six hours if he wished it.

When I went to foment his limbs, I could not find a morsel of flannel. At last I thought of the servant's blanket, and tore it in two. Sir William said this was a most delightful thing, and refreshed him very much. He expressed a great wish to have a bit on his chest. I did not know what to do for flannel. I regretted now excessively not having brought a change of clothes; for

I could have taken a flannel petticoat. This put me in mind of the one I had on, and I instantly tore a great piece out of it and put it into the tub. The cottagers held up their hands, exclaiming, "Ah, madame!" He said it did him good, and was delicious, unconscious where we had found the flannel; indeed he never was aware of the difficulty, for the tub was placed in the outer room.

General Dundas came. Sir William heard me speaking to him, and asked who it was. I told him, and he asked if he was going to remain. I said he was. Sir William seemed gratified, but did not say anything. Surely no earthly feeling can be superior to such perfect sympathy.

Sir William fell asleep, and I went out to see if there was anything for General Dundas to eat. He told me he had got a very good room upstairs, and was willing to remain as long as I wished. His only request was that I would not mind him any more than if he was not there, but send for him when I wanted him. I opened the door of Sir William's room and sat close to it, so as to hear if he moved or spoke. I sat down to coffee for the first meal I had, and talked over several things necessary to be settled with General Dundas. I could not speak above a whisper, my voice was so faint. He entreated me, if possible, to try and take some rest that night, for fear I should be ill before my husband could spare me. I promised.

He then told me that Lady Hamilton had

asked him to take me to her house when I returned to Brussels; and also the Count de Lannoy had prepared rooms, which he begged I would occupy as long as I pleased. I preferred going to the house we had been in before, and I thought I could be more entirely alone there than at any other person's house, which was what I wished, and knew would be best for me. I was struck when I did return to Brussels, with two marks of attention. I had a message from the Commissary to say that orders had been given that I was to draw rations and forage for as long as I stayed; and the other circumstance was this. On the letters I had sent from Antwerp I had neglected to write "private," which is necessary when writing to a person in office. I gave them up for lost, and was uncomfortable. After I had been three days at Brussels, they were all returned unopened from Headquarters.

Sir William called me. I sat a short time beside him, and after I had prepared drink for the night I told him I was so very tired I would go and lie down for a short time, if he would allow my maid to bring the medicine which he took every four hours. He agreed, and asked if I did not always take plenty of sleep.

I said, "Oh yes," and was going, when he said the pain in his chest was returning, and perhaps leeches would do some good. This was the only time I hesitated to oblige him, for I really could scarcely stand; but of course I proceeded to apply the leeches, and in a few minutes the excessive drowsiness went off; so much so, that when after an hour I went to lie down, I could not sleep. I started every moment, thinking he called me. I desired Emma to waken me if he spoke or seemed uneasy. She gave him the medicine. He looked at her, and asked where I was; she told him I was sleeping.

He said, "That's right, quite right."

The pain in his chest grew intolerable, and depending upon my being asleep he yielded to complaint, and groaned very much. Emma roused me and told me she feared he was suffering very much. I had slept half an hour.

I went and stood near him, and he then ceased to complain, and said, "Oh, it was only a little twitch."

I felt at that time as if I was an oppression to him, and I was going away, but he desired me to stay. I sat down and rubbed it, which healed the pain, and towards morning I put on the blister. Between five and six he ate some toasted bread and tea, about two inches of bread. Before he began he entreated me to take off the blister only for ten minutes, that he might eat in tolerable comfort. I said I would take it away entirely, and he was pleased. The doctor came about nine. He was breathing then with great difficulty, and there was a rough sound in his throat. Mr Powell said the only thing to be done was to keep him quiet as usual, and to prevent him speaking. He asked Mr Powell if he might rise, for he might breathe easier at the window, and he was so tired of lying in that bed. Mr Powell urged him not to think of it; he was not able; it would hurt him very much, etc.

About eleven o'clock he sent me away for ten minutes, and with the help of his servant he rose and got to the other end of the room. I was terrified when I heard he was up, and called General Dundas, who went in and found him almost fainting. They placed him in bed again, and when I returned he was much exhausted. I opened the windows wide and shut the door, and sat by him alone, in hopes that he might go to sleep and recover a little. He slept every now and then for a little. He seemed oppressed with the length of the day for the first time. He asked repeatedly what o'clock it was; he often asked if it was three yet. When I told him it was near five, he seemed surprised. At night he said he wished he could fall upon some device to shorten the weary long night; he could not bear it so long. I could not think of any plan. He said if I could lie down beside him it would cut off five or six hours. I said it was impossible, for I was afraid to hurt him, there was so little room. His mind seemed quite bent upon it. Therefore I stood upon a chair and stepped over him, for he could not move an inch, and he lay at the outer edge. He was delighted; and it shortened the night indeed, for we both fell asleep.

At five in the morning I rose. He was very anxious to have his wound dressed; it had never been looked at. He said there was a little pain, merely a trifle, but it teased him. Mr Powell objected; he said it would fatigue him too much that day. He consented to delay. I then washed his face and hands, and brushed his hair, after which I gave him his breakfast. He again wished to rise, but I persuaded him not to do it; he said he would not do anything I was averse to, and he said, "See what control your poor husband is under." He smiled, and drew me so close to him that he could touch my face, and he continued stroking it with his hand for some time.

Towards eleven o'clock he grew more uneasy; he was restless and uncomfortable; his breathing was like choking, and as I sat gazing at him I could distinctly hear the water rattling in his throat. I opened the door and windows to make a draught. I desired the people to leave the outer room, that his might be as quiet as usual; and then I sat down to watch the melancholy progress of the water in his chest, which I saw would soon be fatal.

About three o'clock Dr Hume and Mr Powell came. I must do the former the justice to say he was grave enough now. Sir William repeated his request to have the wound dressed. Dr Hume consented, and they went away to prepare something to wash it with; they remained away half an hour. I sat down by my husband and took his hand; he said he wished I would not look so unhappy. I wept; and he spoke to me with so much affection. He repeated every endearing expression. He bade me kiss him. He called me his dear wife. The surgeons returned. My husband turned on one side with great difficulty; it seemed to give much pain.

After I had brought everything the surgeons wanted, I went into another room. I could not bear to see him suffering. Mr Powell saw a change in his countenance; he looked out, and desired Emma to call me, to tell me instantly Sir William wanted me. I hastened to him, reproaching myself for having been absent a moment.

I stood near my husband, and he looked up at me and said, "Magdalene, my love, the spirits." I stooped down close to him and held the bottle of lavender to him: I also sprinkled some near him. He looked pleased. He gave a little gulp, as if something was in his throat.

The doctor said, "Ah, poor De Lancey! He is gone." I pressed my lips to his, and left the room. I went upstairs, where I remained, unconscious of what was passing, till Emma came to me and said the carriage was ready, and General Dundas advised me to go that evening to Brussels, but I need not hurry myself. I asked her if the room below was empty. She assured me it was; and I went down and remained some time beside the body. There was such perfect peace and placid calm sweetness in his countenance, that I envied him not a little. He was released: I was left to suffer. I then thought I should not suffer long. As I bent over him I felt as if violent grief would disturb his tranquil rest.

These moments that I passed by his lifeless body were awful, and instructive. Their impression will influence my whole life. I left Waterloo with feelings so different from those I had on going to it. Then all was anxious terror that I would not be there in time to see one look, or to hear one word. Now there was nothing imaginary – all was real misery. There now remained not even a chance of happiness, but what depended on the retrospect of better days and duties fulfilled.

As I drove rapidly along the same road, I could not but recall the irritated state I had been in when I had been there before; and the fervent and sincere resolutions I then made, that if I saw him alive, I never would repine.

Since that time I have suffered every shade of sorrow; but I can safely affirm that except the first few days, when the violence of grief is more like delirium than the sorrow of a Christian, I have never felt that my lot was unbearable. I do not forget the perfection of my happiness while it lasted; and I believe there are many who after a long life cannot say they have felt so much of it.

As I expressed some uneasiness to General Dundas at having left the body with none but servants, Colonel Grant at his request went to Waterloo the same evening, and remained till it was brought up next day to Brussels. General Dundas then kindly executed all my orders with respect to the funeral, etc., which took place on Wednesday the 28th, in the cemetery of the Reformed Church. It is about a mile from Brussels, on the road to Louvain. I had a stone placed, with simply his name and the circumstances of his death. I visited his grave on Tuesday, the 4th of July. The burying-ground is in a sweet, quiet, retired spot. A narrow path leads to it from the road. It is quite out of sight among the fields, and no house but the grave-digger's cottage is near. Seeing my interest in that grave, he begged me to let him plant roses round it, and promised I should see it nicely kept when I returned. I am pleased that I saw the grave and the stone; for there were nearly forty other new graves, and not another stone.

At eleven o'clock that same day, I set out for England. That day, three months before, I was married.

M. De L.

COLONEL SIR WILLIAM HOWE DE LANCEY (*c.* 1813).

Two years after the battle, General Alava, a Spanish ambassor with whom William De Lancey had
dined on the night before the battle, remembered:
"The Duke got back to his quarters at Waterloo
about nine or ten at night. The table was laid for
the usual number, while none appeared of the
many of his Staff but Alava and Fremantle. The
Duke said very little, ate hastily and heartily, but
every time the door opened he gave a searching look, evidently in the hope of some of his
valuable Staff approaching. When he had finished
eating, he held up both hands in an imploring at-
titude and said, 'The hand of Almighty God has
been upon me this day"; jumped up, went to his
couch, and was asleep in a moment."

General Alava had the unique experience of being at both the Battles of Waterloo and Trafalgar.
Quoted in *The Autobiography of Sir Harry Smith
1781-1819.*

**An estimated 48,000 men were killed or
wounded in the Battle of Waterloo.**

"June 22. This morning I went to visit the field of battle, which is a little beyond the village of Waterloo, on the plateau of Mont St Jean; but on arrival there the sight was too horrible to behold. I felt sick in the stomach and was obliged to return. The multitude of carcasses, the heaps of wounded men with mangled limbs unable to move, and perishing from not having their wounds dressed or from hunger, as the Allies were, of course, obliged to take their surgeons and waggons with them, formed a spectacle I shall never forget. The wounded, both of the Allies and the French, remain in an equally deplorable state."

Major W. E Frye *After Waterloo: Reminiscences of European Travel 1815-1819.*

Magdalene left Brussels for England on July 4th 1815. Her sister Susan was to marry Major-General Sir Hudson Lowe, who was appointed Governor of St Helena and became in effect Napoleon's chief gaoler.

Magdalene wrote her account of her experiences at Waterloo in 1816 and the following year she returned to Brussels for a brief visit before rebuilding her life.

In 1818, Magdalene fell passionately in love again, this time with Captain Henry Harvey of the Madras Infantry. The couple were married in 1819. Harvey retired from the army and the couple set out on a 'Grand Tour' of Europe. Their first child, Helen, was born in Rome in January 1820. The family grew rapidly as a son, Robert, was born later in the same year. A second daughter, Frances, was born in 1822 but Magdalene failed to recover from the birth and died during a family holiday in the seaside spa of Salcombe Regis on the south-coast of England. She was twenty-eight-years-old. Six years later, her son Robert died, aged eight.

Two of her descendants - her great-grandson and great-great grandson – were to give their lives fighting for their country in World War One and World War Two.

*Magdalene De Lancey's brother, Captain Basil Hall,
who was a well-known author, lent the Narrative to
two of the most famous literary men of the time, Sir
Walter Scott and Charles Dickens.*

ABBOTSFORD, *13th October 1825*.

MY DEAR CAPTAIN HALL,
I received with great pleasure your kind proposal
to visit Tweedside. It arrived later than it should
have done. I lose no time in saying that you and
Mrs Hall cannot come but as welcome guests
any day next week, which may best suit you. If
you have time to drop a line we will make our
dinner hour suit your arrival, but you cannot
come amiss to us.

I am infinitely obliged to you for Captain
Maitland's plain, manly, and interesting narrative.

It is very interesting, and clears Bonaparte of
much egotism imputed to him. I am making a
copy which, however, I will make no use of except as extracts, and am very much indebted to
Captain Maitland for the privilege. Constable
proposed a thing to me which was of so much
delicacy that I scarce know how [sic] about it,
and thought of leaving it till you and I met.

It relates to that most interesting and affecting
journal kept by my regretted and amiable friend,
Mrs Hervey, during poor De Lancey's illness. He

thought with great truth that it would add very
great interest as an addition to the letters which
I wrote from Paris soon after Waterloo, and certainly I would consider it as one of the most
valuable and important documents which could
be published as illustrative of the woes of war.
But whether this could be done without injury
to the feelings of survivors is a question not for
me to decide, and indeed I feel unaffected pain
in even submitting it to your friendly ear who
I know will put no harsh construction upon
my motive which can be no other than such as
would do honour to the amiable and lamented
authoress. I never read anything which affected
my own feelings more strongly or which I am
sure would have a deeper interest on those of
the public. Still the work is of a domestic nature,
and its publication, however honourable to all
concerned, might perhaps give pain when God
knows I should be sorry any proposal of mine
should awaken the distresses which time may
have in some degree abated. You are the only
person who can judge of this with any certainty
or at least who can easily gain the means of as-
certaining it, and as Constable seemed to think
there was a possibility that after the lapse of so
much time it might be regarded as matter of history and as a record of the amiable character of
your accomplished sister, and seemed to suppose
there was some probability of such a favour be-

ing granted, you will consider me as putting the question on his suggestion. It could be printed as the Journal of a lady during the last illness of a General Officer of distinction during her attendance upon his last illness, or something to that purpose. Perhaps it may be my own high admiration of the contents of this heartrending diary which makes me suppose a possibility that after such a lapse of years, the publication may possibly (as that which cannot but do the highest honour to the memory of the amiable authoress) may not be judged altogether inadmissible. You may and will, of course, act in this matter with your natural feeling of consideration, and ascertain whether that which cannot but do honour to the memory of those who are gone can be made public with the sacred regard due to the feelings of survivors.

Lady Scott begs to add the pleasure she must have in seeing Mrs Hall and you at Abbotsford, and in speedy expectation of that honour I am always,

Dear Sir,
Most truly yours,
WALTER SCOTT.

DEVONSHIRE TERRACE,
Tuesday evening 16th March 1841.

MY DEAR HALL,
For I see it must be 'juniores priores,' and that I must demolish the ice at a blow.

I have not had courage until last night to read Lady De Lancey's narrative, and, but for your letter, I should not have mastered it even then. One glance at it, when through your kindness it first arrived, had impressed me with a foreboding of its terrible truth, and I really have shrunk from it in pure lack of heart.

After working at Barnaby all day, and wandering about the most wretched and distressful streets for a couple of hours in the evening – searching for some pictures I wanted to build upon – I went at it, at about ten o'clock. To say that the reading that most astonishing and tremendous account has constituted an epoch in my life – that I shall never forget the lightest word of it – that I cannot throw the impression aside, and never saw anything so real, so touching, and so actually present before my eyes, is nothing. I am husband and wife, dead man and living woman, Emma and General Dundas, doctor and bedstead everything and everybody (but the Prussian officer damn him) all in one. What I have always looked upon as masterpieces of powerful and affecting description, seem as nothing in my eyes.

If I live for fifty years, I shall dream of it every now and then, from this hour to the day of my death, with the most frightful reality. The slightest mention of a battle will bring the whole thing before me. I shall never think of the Duke any more, but as he stood in his shirt with the officer in full-dress uniform, or as he dismounted from his horse when the gallant man was struck down.

It is a striking proof of the power of that most extraordinary man, Defoe, that I seem to recognise in every line of the narrative something of him. Has this occurred to you? The going to Waterloo with that unconsciousness of everything in the road, but the obstacles to getting on - the shutting herself up in her room and determining not to hear - the not going to the door when the knocking came - the finding out by her wild spirits when she heard he was safe, how much she had feared when in doubt and anxiety - the desperate desire to move towards him - the whole description of the cottage, and its condition; and their daily shifts and contrivances ; and the lying down beside him in the bed and both *falling asleep* ; and his resolving not to serve any more, but to live quietly thenceforth; and her sorrow when she saw him eating with an appetite, so soon before his death ; and his death itself - all these are matters of truth, which only that astonishing creature, as I think, could have told in fiction.

Of all the beautiful and tender passages - the

thinking every day how happy and blest she was
– the decorating him for the dinner – the standing in the balcony at night and seeing the troops
melt away through the gate – and the rejoining
him on his sick bed – I say not a word. They are
God's own, and should be sacred. But let me say
again, with an earnestness which pen and ink can
no more convey than toast and water, in thank-
ing you heartily for the perusal of this paper,
that its impression on me can never be told; that
the ground she travelled (which I know well) is
holy ground to me from this day; and that, please
Heaven, I will tread its every foot this very next
summer, to have the softened recollection of this
sad story on the very earth where it was acted.

You won't smile at this, I know. When my en-
thusiasms are awakened by such things they don't
wear out.

Have you ever thought within yourself of
that part where, having suffered so much by the
news of his death, she *will not* believe he is alive?
I should have supposed that unnatural if I had
seen it in fiction.

I shall never dismiss the subject from my mind,
but with these hasty and very imperfect words I
shall dismiss it from my paper, with two addition-
al remarks – firstly, that Kate has been grievously
putting me out by sobbing over it, while I have
been writing this, and has just retired in an agony
of grief; and, secondly, that *if* a time *should* ever

come when you would not object to letting a
friend copy it for himself, I hope you will bear
me in your thoughts.

It seems the poorest nonsense in the world
to turn to anything else, that is, seems to me being fresher in respect of Lady De Lancey than
you - but my raven's dead. He had been ailing
for a few days but not seriously, as we thought,
and was apparently recovering, when symptoms
of relapse occasioned me to send for an eminent
medical gentleman one Herring (a bird fancier
in the New Road), who promptly attended and
administered a powerful dose of castor oil. This
was on Tuesday last. On Wednesday morning he
had another dose of castor oil and a tea cup full
of warm gruel, which he took with great relish
and under the influence of which he so far recovered his spirits as to be enabled to bite the groom
severely. At 12 o' clock at noon he took several
turns up and down the stable with a grave, sedate
air, and suddenly reeled. This made him thought-
ful. He stopped directly, shook his head, moved
on again, stopped once more, cried in a tone of
remonstrance and considerable surprise, 'Halloa
old girl!' and immediately died.

He has left a rather large property (in cheese
and halfpence) buried, for security's sake, in
various parts of the garden. I am not without
suspicions of poison. A butcher was heard to
threaten him some weeks since, and he stole a

clasp knife belonging to a vindictive carpenter, which was never found. For these reasons, I directed a post-mortem examination, preparatory to the body being stuffed; the result of it has not yet reached me. The medical gentleman broke out the fact of his decease to me with great delicacy, observing that 'the jolliest queer start had taken place with that 'ere knowing card of a bird, as ever he see'd' – but the shock was naturally very great. With reference to the jollity of the start, it appears that a raven dying at two hundred and fifty or thereabouts, is looked upon as an infant. This one would hardly, as I may say, have been born for a century or so to come, being only two or three years old.

I want to know more about the promised 'tickler' – when it's to come, what it's to be, and in short all about it – that I may give it the better welcome. I don't know how it is, but I am celebrated either for writing no letters at all or for the briefest specimens of epistolary correspondence in existence, and here I am – in writing to you – on the sixth side! I won't make it a seventh anyway; so with love to all your home circle, and from all mine, I am now and always,

Faithfully yours,
CHARLES DICKENS.
I am glad you like Barnaby. I have great designs in store, but am sadly cramped at first for room.

DONATION

Part of the profits from this book go to the Army Families Federation (AFF), which is the independent voice of Army families and works hard to improve the quality of life for Army families around the world.

AFF are often pivotal in achieving improvements for Army families, such as changes to Government and military policy and changes to the delivery of how services are provided for families. The AFF does not do this by itself; its role is to highlight problems to the chain of command or service providers, and to work with them and other agencies to improve the support they provide for Army families.

AFF also provides a signposting service to help families find the right person to speak to; it intervenes in individual case studies, and supplies useful information for Army families through its website (www.aff.org.uk) and magazine, the AFF Families Journal.